I0102076

What's The Deal With Long-Term Care?

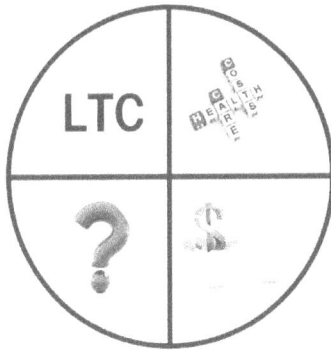

by
Mike Padawer

Copyright 2013 by Mike Padawer
ISBN: 978-0-9850820-7-9

All rights reserved. No part of this book shall be reproduced, stored in a retrieval system, or transmitted by any means, electronic, mechanical, photocopying, recording, or otherwise, without written permission from the publisher. No patent liability is assumed with respect to the use of this information contained herein. Although every precaution has been taken in the preparation of this book, the publisher and author assume no responsibility for errors or omissions. Neither is any liability assumed for damages resulting from the use of information contained herein. For information, contact us at People Tested Books, 123 Broemel Place #815, Pennington, NJ 08534.

The author and publisher specifically disclaim any responsibility for any liability, loss, or risk, personal or otherwise, which is incurred as a consequence, directly or indirectly, of the use and application of any of the contents of this book.

This book makes no financial recommendations to the reader and should not be viewed as a substitute for the need to review this topic with a trusted advisor, resource or expert.

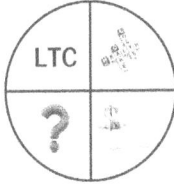

Table of Contents

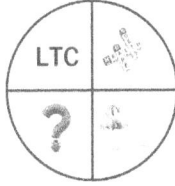

Preface
By Jack Tatar

One of the benefits of being the publisher and owner of People Tested Publications is that I can suggest titles for our **"What's the Deal with.."** series of books. This book that you're reading was based on one of those suggestions and I'm glad that Mike has decided to write this book.

For those familiar with my books including "*Having the Talk: The Four Keys to Your Parents' Safe Retirement*,"[1] it will come as no surprise that discussing Long-Term Care is a necessary part of any retirees' plan. As we move forward into a world of increasing healthcare costs, uncertainty about health insurance plans and a need to preserve the assets that we've worked hard for, the need to discuss and evaluate Long-Term Care as an option in your financial plans is even more critical.

When I met Mike Padawer, I knew that I had the right person to write this book. Mike runs an advisory firm that specializes in advising not only retirees and their families on Long-Term Care options and plans, but financial advisors as well. He understands the importance of considering

---

1 Jack's books are available on Amazon at http://Jack.PeopleTested.com

Long-Term Care plans for individuals, and he also under-stands that there is a lot of confusion, skepticism and outright misinformation in the marketplace on this topic as well.

That's why he has spent his career educating and assisting individuals, families and advisors on this topic so that everyone can make an educated and thorough decision on this important topic.

We're fortunate that Mike has distilled his knowledge and approach to Long-Term Care planning into this book. The intent of this book is not to provide you with everything you need to know about Long-Term Care plans, but rather to give you what you need so that you can have an informed and knowledgeable discussion with a trusted advisor who can find the best solution for you and your own situation.

You should never make a final decision on something as important as Long-Term Care from reading a book. The only decision that you should make after reading this book is whether or not you'll have that discussion with an advisor about this important topic.

Mike has not only included his expertise into the pages of this book but he's provided resources that will help you to move forward on learning more about the topic and taking the next steps.

I can speak from my own experience that the decision and discussions about Long-Term Care planning are often complex and stressful. They involve thinking about the possibility that you or a loved one may become incapacitated and require extensive care in your later years. They also include the reality of how the costs for this care can not only deplete the assets that you've worked hard for, but how these costs can disrupt even the best designed financial plans and turn your heirs' assets into paying for long term facilities.

When I considered Long-Term Care for my wife and I, we were stunned at the costs and complexity involved. I was also fortunate to have a trusted advisor who was knowledgeable about the subject and knew my situation very well. Although it took him much time to educate us and answer all of our questions, his patience and direction paid off.

At the end of the process, I was amazed at the feeling that we came away with after my wife and I had made our decision on Long-Term Care solutions; it was the feeling of "peace of mind" that we had.

I hope that all of you who read this book will not only benefit from Mike's knowledge and resources, but that it helps to lead you to a place where you too, can have "peace of mind" on a topic that has become so important and necessary to discuss and evaluate—Long-Term Care planning.

Fortunately for you, you have something that I didn't have—this book.

Jack Tatar is author of three books that are changing how people view retirement.

His first, "Safe 4 Retirement: The Four Keys to a Safe Retirement"[2] lays out his foundational approach to viewing retirement in a holistic fashion by including the Four Keys: Financial Preparedness, Health & Wellness, Mental Attitude and Staying Involved into plans for retirement.

2 http://www.Safe.PeopleTested.com

His second book, "The 10 Joys of a Safe Retirement"[3] examines the way that living longer and thriving in retirement can bring joy to your life, and to those around you. His latest book is "Having The Talk: The Four Keys to Your Parents' Safe Retirement"[4], which lays out the need and plan for having that necessary "talk" between retired or retiring parents, and their children and family about later life issues. He writes regularly for Marketwatch.com as one of their RetireMentors.[5]

He can be reached at Jack@Safe4Retirement.com

---

3 http://www.Joys.PeopleTested.com

4 http://www.Talk.PeopleTested.com

5 http://www.marketwatch.com/retirement/mentors/stories?authorid=21194

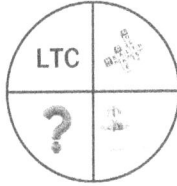

What's The Deal With Long-Term Care?

Death, Taxes, and Rising Healthcare Costs

We all know the saying "*nothing in life is certain except death and taxes*", but maybe it's time to modify it to "*nothing in life is certain except death, taxes and rising health care costs*?"

Based on almost everything you read or hear today, a majority of Americans agree with my revision. Whether this applies to you, your parents or other family members, it's time to face reality and begin planning for a future full of unknowns—including rising healthcare costs.

Fidelity Investments issued their annual study on health-care cost and concluded that "*a 65-year-old couple retiring in 2013 is estimated to need $220,000 to cover medical expenses throughout retirement*" and "*households relying on Social Security benefits to cover these costs should expect medical bills to consume 61% of their social security payments by 2027.*" What's even more concerning is the fact that the study "*does not include any costs associated with nursing-home* *care and applies to retirees with traditional Medicare insurance coverage.*"[6]

Usually, discussions about healthcare costs in retirement focus solely on Medicare, as this is the primary insurance coverage for Americans over age 65. However, I strongly encourage people to gain a better understanding of what Medicare actually covers, especially since some of the most expensive healthcare services facing retirees will be those associated with Long-Term Care.

Long-Term Care includes a variety of services, which help meet both the medical and non-medical needs of those with a chronic illness or disability, or who cannot care for themselves for long periods of time. It is common for Long-Term Care to provide custodial and non-skilled care, such as assisting with normal daily tasks like dressing, bathing, and using the bathroom. Increasingly, Long-Term Care involves providing a level of medical care that requires the expertise of skilled practitioners to address the often multiple, chronic conditions associated with older populations.

Long-Term Care can be provided at home, in the community, in assisted living facilities or in nursing homes. Although Long-Term Care may be needed by people of any age, it is a more common need for individuals in their later years.

Unfortunately, most Americans relying on Medicare mistakenly believe Long-Term Care is covered; when in reality, it's not!

Not only is Long-Term Care one of the most misunderstood elements of healthcare costs, it's also one of the largest

---

6 Fidelity Investments: "*Retiree health costs fall*", https://www.fidelity.com/viewpoints/retirees-medical-expenses, May 15, 2013

potential financial risks that all Americans face. According to Kevin McGarry, director of the Nationwide Institute for Retirement Income, *"one reason people may underestimate the amount of money needed to cover their health care costs in retirement is that many workers do not think they will ever need long-term care."*[7]

Unfortunately, he's correct, and even those with optimistic views of the future should recognize the need for a more proactive approach to this issue. For those turning 65 right now, the statistics vary on what percentage will need care and for how long. But, according to the Employee Benefit Research Institute, 30 to 40 percent of those reaching age 65 will use nursing home care at some point.[8] Taking it a step further, when you include home health care, assisted living or community based care for retirees, the U.S. Department of Health & Human Services estimates that 70% of Americans will experience the need for Long-Term Care services.[9]

Another report, which appears in the Journal of General Internal Medicine, surveyed 3,209 Medicare beneficiaries from 2002 to 2008. Their findings illustrate the financial ramifications of this issue: average out-of-pocket expenditures in the five years prior to death were $38,688 for individuals and $51,030 for couples. This is primarily due to the costs associated with Long-Term Care needs. The final paragraph of the report puts things into perspective: *"As more Baby Boomers retire, a new generation of widows or widowers could face*

---

7 Nationwide Insurance: *"Study: Nearly half of soon-to-be-retired, high-net-worth Americans "terrified" of health care costs in retirement"*, May 7, 2013

8 Employee Benefit Research Institute: *"Effects of Nursing Home Stays on Household Portfolios"*, June 2012, Issue #372

9 U.S. Department of Health and Human Services website, http://longtermcare. gov/the-basics/who-needs-care/

a sharply diminished financial future as they confront their recently-depleted nest egg following the illness and death of a spouse." [10]

While no one can control the rising cost of healthcare, it is possible to put yourself in a position to mitigate future financial risks associated with healthcare. For most Americans though, simply putting money aside will not be sufficient to offset rising healthcare and Long-Term Care costs.

It's likely that you envision yourself living a long life, investing and planning to create a financially secure future where you can enjoy retirement by spending time doing the things that you enjoy the most.

If this is your goal, your **COMPREHENSIVE** retirement, financial, estate or risk management plan should address the impact that Long-Term Care may have on your planning, your family, and your future.

This book will help you to understand the issues surrounding Long-Term Care, and how to secure your financial future by including a Long-Term Care component in your financial and retirement plans for yourself and your family.

---

10 Journal of General Internal Medicine: *"Healthcare costs hit the elderly hard, diminish financial well being"*, September 4, 2012

What's The Impact of Needing Long-Term Care?

The Financial Impact

The reality is that the longer you live, the greater the likelihood is that you will require Long-Term Care services. The costs associated with needing Long-Term Care are significant, and while it can take decades to accumulate the assets you'll need to retire comfortably, just a few years of paying for Long-Term Care may significantly threaten your lifetime of savings.

Modern medicine has taken us to the point where the illnesses and diseases which once ended a life, no longer do. However, while the longevity of the body may be extended, illnesses affecting the mind are a completely different story.

According to the Alzheimer's Association, "*in 2013, the direct costs of caring for those with Alzheimer's to American society will total an estimated $203 billion, and this number is expected to rise to $1.2 trillion by 2050.*" [11] There are an

---

11 Alzheimer's Association—Fact and Figures: http://www.alz.org/alzheimers_disease_facts_and_figures.asp

estimated 5.2 million Americans suffering from the disease, which is now the 6th leading cause of death in our country.

From the perspective of Long-Term Care planning, last year claims for reimbursement citing Alzheimer's as the primary diagnosis topped $6.6 billion for more than 200,000 with coverage. "*The rate of spending is unsustainable*," says Jesse Slome, Executive Director, and American Association for Long-Term Care Insurance. Slome goes on to state that "*if people are concerned about the future availability of government resources for the costs of care, that implementing a Long-Term Care Plan in advance of a diagnosis is very important.*"[12]

As a country, we face the unfortunate reality of an aging population, which is either unable or unwilling to see what may be in their future. Research and treatment for Alzheimer's, and other dementia related illnesses, is far behind the curve, and the enormity of the numbers associated with Alzheimer's projections is just one of the myriad of issues which will increase the cost of healthcare.

The Unseen Burden of Caregiving

With 10,000 Baby Boomers turning 65 everyday,[13] what's even more distressing is the fact that, in addition to the financial burden, even fewer people realize the significant *physical and emotional* burden associated with Long-Term Care needs. Whether you're engaged in financial planning for yourself, or work with an advisor, it's important to understand who's carrying the burden of providing care.

12 American Association for Long-Term Care Insurance, "*Alzheimer's Disease Is Top Long-Term Care Insurance Claim*", July 19th, 2012
13 Pew Research Center, "*Baby Boomers Retire*", December 29, 2010

If you've ever been in a caregiving situation, you understand the physical and emotional toll it can take. While providing care to loved ones is an act of compassion, placing these burdens on spouses, children and other family members can create a significant emotional and physical strain, and is something that many people would like to avoid.

From mundane tasks like mowing the grass and landscaping, to more complicated ones like electrical work or remodeling, "Honey-Do List" items are often things many Americans would like to avoid. Unfortunately, as we age, even simple chores can become difficult or even impossible to complete, and this is when Family Caregiving and/or Long-Term Care services are often required.

Consider a recent report by CBS News in Boston that highlights the issue by stating that boomers "will likely spend more years caring for a parent than for their children." Although they're in the prime of their lives, Americans "in their 50s are now caring for parents who are in their 70s and 80s."[14]

And the boomers often had children later in life so they fall into what's known as the "Sandwich Generation".[15] This is the situation where their parents may need them to help pay the bills, grocery shop and drive them places and their teenagers need them to pay the bills, keep them in groceries and chauffeur them around as well.

This isn't a new phenomenon, as families have always been providing care for the older generation. However, according to the National Alliance for Caregiving, the trend

14 CBS News, Boston, "*How to Help Dad This Father's Day*" June 10, 2013
15 MSN Money, "*Surviving the sandwich generation*", March 30, 2012

in the United States paints an alarming picture of a growing problem:

1) There are 43.5 million caregivers age 18 and over, equivalent to 19 percent of all adults, who provide unpaid care to an adult family member or friend who is age 50 years or older.

2) Caregivers are overwhelming female (67%) and average 50 years of age.

3) More than half (55%) are providing care and still work full-time.

4) Most of the care is being provided for chronic or age-related conditions where Medicare doesn't cover LTC expenses.[16]

There are also disturbing trends regarding the economic impact of providing care. Researchers from Rice University released data that "shows in all 50 states, including Washington D.C., that families with members having disabilities (including illness), live in poverty at a higher rate. In fact, the same research shows that female family caregivers are 2.5 times more likely to live in poverty than non-caregivers, and caregiving households have more than a 15 percent lower income than non-caregiving households."[16]

The difficult economic environment, since 2008, has amplified the financial problem. In fact, 20% of caregivers had to move in with those that they were caring for, in order to reduce expenses, as reported by the National Alliance for

---

16 *Rice University, Data compiled from the Health and Retirement Study funded by the National Institute of Aging and conducted by the University of Michigan, 1992-2004*

Caregiving. And, despite efforts to reduce expenses, 47% of working caregivers report continuing increased expenses caused them to use all or most of their savings, which has a direct impact on the financial security and retirement plans for these caregivers.[17]

For the average family caregiver who is caring for someone over the age of 50, that caregiver is on average spending $5,531 per year, out of pocket, for expenses not covered by insurance or Medicare. This is more than 10 percent of the average income for caregivers, according to the Congressional Research Service.[18]

Maybe the next time mom or dad mentions that they need your help with their "honey-do list", consider that your cue to consider the day when their chores, or overall care, may ultimately become your responsibility...

This should help put Long-Term Care planning into an even better perspective, and should make it clear why this should be an important component of any financial or retirement plan.

The Consequences of Not Having a Plan

Are you like so many others who are still waiting to address your long-term care needs?

The reality is that the longer you wait, it may significantly impact your current and future financial situation. If you decide to wait until the point at which you actually need care, it WILL be too late and you will realize not only a significant impact

---

17 ibid

18 Kirsten J. Costello, Congressional Research Service, "Family Caregiving to Older Population: Background, Federal Programs and Issues for Congress", January 29, 2009

on your financial situation but on your quality of life and your ability to maintain your independence as well.

Incorporating a Long-Term Care component in a comprehensive financial plan can help protect your assets, reduce the burdens that could fall onto family members, and enable you to receive care in the setting that you most prefer, including your own home.

Once you understand the risks associated with needing long-term care, you should be ready to start the planning process. As you weigh your decision to begin Long-Term Care Planning, there are a variety of factors to consider.

These include even the most basic factors, such as where you plan to live when you retire, the settings you would prefer to receive care and how much of your Long-Term Care expenses are you willing, or able, to pay out of your own pocket.

Finally, there is another important reason to address your potential Long-Term Care needs, sooner rather than later. Since the cost of implementing a Long-Term Care plan is based on your age and health, the older you are when you begin the process, the higher your costs will be.

The Changing American Family

Another key planning point is family dynamics, as American families have become more diverse than ever before. With respect to trends in Long-Term Care Planning, a little over half of Long-Term Care plans today are for couples—representing 54% of the new plans implemented. However, there are more non-traditional family models today than ever before.[19]

19 Prudential Insurance Company, "Long-Term Care Insurance: A Piece of the Retirement & Estate Planning Puzzle", 2011

This includes the multitude of retirees today who are divorced, widowed, never-married, same-sex couples, etc. Regardless of where you fit into these categories, Long-Term Care will likely impact you and your family, so appropriate planning is very important.

Women, overall, are more likely to need Long-Term Care,[20] so it's not uncommon for some couples to look to address the greater risk for a couple. However, this approach may create a far greater financial risk and emotional toll should a husband need care prior to his spouse. Regardless of which one is not covered, the risk of needing care and the subsequent caregiving and financial responsibilities that follow will impact the couple's quality of life and financial situation.

Singles, or those in non-traditional family units, face a different set of planning variables, as there may be no built-in caregiver to lean on. This means that expenses for Long-Term Care should be expected earlier, and in a potentially more expansive way, than that for couples.

In decades past, it was fairly common to see multiple generations living under one roof; where caregiving might be accomplished by using a "team" approach. But, as times have changed, and families are spread out across cities or the country, this is usually not a viable option.

For those attempting it today, they often find themselves as part of the "Sandwich Generation", where they're providing

---

20 Excellus Health Plan, Inc., Long-Term Care Over An Uncertain Future: What Can Current Retirees Expect?", by Peter Kemper, PhD (Department of Health Policy and Administration, The Pennsylvania State University), Harriet Komisar, PhD.(Health Policy Institute, Georgetown University) and Lisa Alecxih, PhD (Vice President, The Lewin Group), Volume 42, Winter 2005/2006

support not only for their aging parents but even their adult children.

According to a recent Pew Research poll, "*Americans believe overwhelmingly that adult children are obligated to provide financial assistance to an aging parent if needed: 75% say this is a responsibility, 23% say it is not.*"[21] In any event, this scenario can have unforeseen consequences which will effect each generation involved.

Another fast growing American family unit are those in the Lesbian-Gay-Bisexual-Transgender (LGBT) Community, and as with other groups, they are finding the need for Long-Term Care planning as a valuable and necessary financial planning tool. Not only can a Long-Term Care plan help them and their partners avoid the stress and burden of caregiving, it can eliminate some of the issues unique to their needs.

According to a recent article in the Boston Globe, "*an estimated 4-8 percent of seniors today identify themselves as LGBT and the percentage is expected to double by 2030, according to the National Gay and Lesbian Task Force, as LGBT baby boomers, who are more likely to be open about their sexual orientation, age. For many LGBT seniors, their biggest concern now is not trying to conform to an unwelcoming society, but rather, who will care for them as they get older. They are less likely to have ever been married or have children, leaving them without a close relative to take on the role of caregiver*".[22]

---

21 Pew Research Center, "*The Sandwich Generation Rising Financial Burdens for Middle-Aged Americans*", January 30, 2013

22 Lara Salahi, The Boston Globe, "*Learning how to care for LGBT seniors*", December 10, 2012

Although times and laws are changing, many in the LGBT community will still find themselves subject to legal issues not faced by heterosexual individuals and couples. They also have specific concerns with respect to aging, as one recent study of gay and lesbian participants over age 40, found that more than 70% reported concerns about the ability to care for themselves in the future.[23] Thus, Long-Term Care Planning will help fill a potential caregiving gap, while allowing individuals and partners to receive care in the familiar surroundings of home or location of their own choosing.

As LGBT couples plan for the future and begin to prepare for the next phase of their life together, the reality is that they are no different from others who need to consider the financial, physical, and emotional impacts of Long-Term Care.

23 Prudential Insurance Company, "*The LGBT Financial experience: 2012-2013 Prudential Research Study*", November 2012

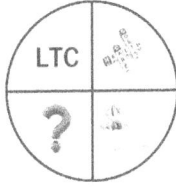

What Are The Greatest Myths About Long-Term Care?

While there are many ways to break down the demographics, perhaps it's best to realize that every demographic has unfortunately bought into the myths regarding Long-Term Care. The most common one is that most can "self-insure" for their future Long-Term Care expenses.

Unfortunately, those who take this route are relying on some type of government program to help along the way. Yet, with continued gridlock and partisan bickering in Washington D.C., should anyone *really* expect to depend on politicians to address their future Long-Term Care needs?

The 2012 election opened debate about the future our country, and a variety of important issues were raises such as Social Security, Medicare and Medicaid—the "Third Rail" of politics. It's easy to see why these programs are the "800 lb. gorilla" in the room when you consider their ongoing and future costs, along with federal debt that now tops $17 trillion.[24] It seems safe to say that one way or another, there are probably some changes on the way.

Regardless of your political bent, it's impossible to believe that our country can maintain our spending trajectory for Medicare, Medicaid and Social Security in its current form. I'm not going to argue the merits of the solutions presented by either party, but when it comes to dealing with future Long-Term Care expenses, the unfortunate reality is that there are already gaping holes in that safety net.

There seems to be little that the government can do to fix the current problem, as neither party has even presented a proposal to address it in the future. This means it is now time for you and/or your family, to gain a better understanding of Medicare, Medicaid and Social Security, with respect to Long-Term Care concerns, which you are more than likely to encounter in your/their future.

It's important to recognize that Medicare has very limited provisions with respect to covering Long-Term Care expenses. The truth is that relying on Medicare really isn't a viable "solution" and the Medicare website is the easiest place to verify that fact.[25]

If you need another reference point, consider the Social Security statement you used to receive each year. The government stopped sending those statements simply because of the high cost of doing so, but I would encourage you to set up an account with the Social Security Administration so you can view your current benefit projections.[26]

---

24 US Debt Clock, http://www.usdebtclock.org/

25 Medicare.gov, "*What's not covered by Part A & Part B?*", http://www.medicare.gov/what-medicare-covers/not-covered/item-and-services-not-covered-by-part-a-and-b.html

26 Official Social Security Website, http://www.ssa.gov/myaccount/

Once you register, view your statement and skip to page four, where you will read that "***Medicare does not pay for long-term care, so you may want to consider options for private insurance.***" Whether or not the government makes ANY changes to the current programs, both Medicare and the Social Security Administration makes the point regarding LONG-TERM CARE planning crystal clear!

OK, so if Medicare isn't going to help you, what about Medicaid as an alternative?

First, you should understand that Medicaid is considered to be part of the "welfare system"[27] and it has its own limitation on what Long-Term Care is covered, where it's covered and how it's covered. The Medicaid program *today* will cover Long-Term Care needs, but only after you've exhausted nearly all of your assets. Recognize that the key part of the last sentence is the word "***today***"!! Given the political environment in Washington, D.C. and ever-mounting government debt, I wouldn't count on Medicaid to cover your Long-Term Care needs ***in the future***.

For a moment, assume that you're going to rely on Medicaid to cover your Long-Term Care needs. Now, consider the economic reality of senior care for a moment and the availability of a "Medicaid bed". If you feel that Medicaid could be part of your future, three realities should be realized—(1) You're giving up much of the control of your care, (2) limited control on where you receive that care and (3) you intend on becoming destitute (you no longer have any assets).

Without a Long-Term Care plan of your own, you are essentially "self-insuring" all of your risk of paying for care.

---

27 http://www.thepeoplesview.net/2012/08/medicare-is-welfare-and-so-is-social. html

Whether people overestimate their ability to pay for care over an extended period, or convince themselves that they'll never need care, the risk of needing and paying for care still remains.

Regardless of one's income or level of assets, having a Long-Term Care plan to transfer one of the biggest financial threats you may face can be a smart move towards protecting your assets and those of your loved ones.

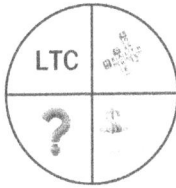

What's The Economic Reality of Long-Term Care?

When you woke up this morning, 10,000 Baby Boomers just turned 65, and this will continue to occur every day for about the next 18 years.[28] As previously mentioned, roughly 70% will experience the need for Long-Term Care at some point in their lives.[29] The degree and duration for which they'll need care remains in question, however the sheer size of this group will significantly impact the delivery of Long-Term Care services, and the economics of the healthcare industry as a whole.

According to Ken Dychtwald, president and CEO of the consulting firm AgeWave, *"anyone who thinks the boomers will turn 65 and be the same as the generation before are missing out on the last 60 years of sociology. The boomers change every stage of life through which they migrate. We weren't prepared for the boomers. There weren't enough hospitals or pediatricians. There weren't enough bedrooms in our*

---

28 Pew Research Center, "*Baby Boomers Retire*", December 29, 2010
29 U.S. Department of Health and Human Services website, http://longtermcare. gov/the-basics/who-needs-care/

homes. There weren't enough schoolteachers or textbooks or playgrounds. The huge size of this generation has strained institutions every step of the way."[30]

It's clear that boomers will have a significant impact on the healthcare system, especially once it's understood how and where their care will likely be provided. While it may be difficult to simplify this complex topic, we'll attempt to do so by looking at three aspects of the healthcare system: *Physicians, Home Health Care and Facility-Based Care.*

Doctors Understand Economics 101

In the not-so-distant future, demand for healthcare (and Long-Term Care services) may very well outstrip available supply, regardless of who provides care or where it's provided. No matter how Washington D.C. tweaks Medicare and Medicaid, or implements the Patient Protection and Affordable Care Act (Obamacare), healthcare providers won't necessarily choose to participate *if the economics of doing so don't make sense.*

Unfortunately, there seems to be no easy way that our politicians can, or will, effectively address issues with Medicare and Medicaid. Even if changes are made, government cannot simply legislate its way around the laws of supply and demand. They can not avoid the economic reality that *supply-side issues* will then dictate price and/or availability. With respect to Medicare and Medicaid, many healthcare providers will embrace basic economic reality: *They have the ability to "opt out" of providing care under the reimbursement terms of government programs.* It's beginning to happen already.

---

30 Laura Rowley, The Huffington Post, "*Baby Boomers will transform aging in America, panel says*", April 2, 2012

A recent *Business Week* article highlights the trend of healthcare providers creating "concierge" practices. "*There aren't enough primary-care people around now*," says Arthur Caplan, director of medical ethics at the NYU Langone Medical Center. "*When concierge practices spread, that means more and more people will be left without any access to primary care*." Furthermore, by 2020, the Association of American Medical Colleges estimates, there will be 45,000 fewer primary-care doctors than the U.S. needs. "*For the last 13 years, very few students have been going into it*," says Patrick Dowling, chairman of the department of family medicine at the University of California-Los Angeles's David Geffen School of Medicine. [31]

Based on supply and demand, Americans may be forced to re-evaluate their expectations as to how healthcare is delivered. If the delivery of healthcare—*through primary-care physicians*—evolves as *Business Week* details,[32] the landscape may change throughout the healthcare system. This could, and likely will, have a direct effect on the delivery and availability of Long-Term Care services as well.

Home Health Care— Maintaining Independence & Choice

Americans love having choices; such as where we live, what we eat, how we entertain ourselves, etc. We are also very selective with respect to our healthcare. Even if you dismiss the possibility of shortages of physicians in the future, or the potential for a two-tiered delivery system of healthcare, it's

---

31 Devin Leonard, Bloomberg Businessweek, "*Is Concierge Medicine the Future of Health Care?*" November 29, 2012

32 bid

impossible to ignore the fact that every American has a desire to age gracefully and independently—*and in their own familiar surroundings.*

This means the preference for home and/or community based care will continue to become more prevalent. As such, there will be a substantial increase in the demand for those providing care in this manner. Once again, increasing demand will likely impact cost and/or the availability of care.

According to the University of California, Center for California Health Workforce Studies, "*there are shortages in the nation's health workforce, particularly among nurses, nursing assistants, home care aides, and personal care workers*" and "*it is important to understand the relationship between the demand for services, the settings in which services will be delivered, and the workforce needed to provide those services.*" [33]

In a much more direct way, Shawn Rimerman, owner of ComForcare Senior Services in St. Louis, MO, illustrates the problem we face. According to Shawn, "*we go to great lengths to screen our caregivers and finding the right people to work for us, who 1) can care for our clients in the way we expect; and 2) who will do so under today's economic model is a huge challenge. The demand and the marketplace dictate what we can charge for those services, and simply put, our biggest cost is paying our caregivers a fair hourly rate. As the aging of our population continues, the onus will fall on individuals and families to meet their needs for Long-Term Care services. Realistically, the financial burden of doing so without having to*

---

33 University of California, San Francisco, Center for California Health Workforce Studies, "*An Aging U.S. Population and the Health Care Workforce: Factors Affecting the Need for Geriatric Care Workers*", February 2006

deplete one's life savings cannot be met through any current or potential government program."[34]

Facility-Based Care:
The Good, The Bad & The Ugly

Most people who need medical attention or Long-Term Care services try to avoid facility-based care. Unfortunately, my experience has shown me that because of certain "flaws" with Medicare and Medicaid reimbursement, the reality is that neither program allows for much flexibility, and therefore, facility-based care becomes the norm. This is typically NOT what the patient wants, and it's very expensive for the system overall.

For example, I recently met with a consumer who described a situation where her husband was recovering from surgery and infections developed during his recovery. Her husband was forced to move to a Long-Term Care facility where he spent 30 days receiving drug therapy to fight the infections. The only service provided by the facility was a daily visit by a nurse to re-fill the intravenous solution containing the medication. In this instance, Medicare could have saved more than $6,000 had the treatment been allowed in their home, and administered by a private-duty nurse. *And this is happening all around the country*!!

Today, government programs enforce out-dated restrictions defining what care can and cannot be provided outside of a medical facility. The lack of cost containment dramatically affects the cumulative cost of healthcare through these

34 INERTIA / Advisor Services Group, "*Long-Term Care: The Economic Reality*", June 19, 2013

programs overall. Tomorrow, another 10,000 Boomers turn 65 and this problem will continue to grow!

The Kaiser Family Foundation, a non-profit foundation, focusing on the major health care issues facing the U.S, compiles a variety of statistics annually. When you analyze some of the figures, they highlight a somewhat nightmarish scenario. Consider the following statistics:

- There are total of 15,622 Nursing Facilities in the United States.

- The total beds in those facilities equal 1,663,445.

- The occupancy rate for those facilities is currently 83.3%.

- The primary payer for 63% of the residents is currently Medicaid.

- Of the 15,622 facilities, 68% operated on a "for-profit" basis.

- Based on current occupancy, this leaves 300,000 beds "available".[35]

Taken alone, these statistics paint a grim picture. Now combine them with the government's Medicare estimates that by 2020 there will be roughly 20 million people accessing some form of Long-Term Care services.[36]

35 State Health Facts, The Kaiser Family Foundation, "*Certified Nursing Facility Beds*", http://kff.org/other/state-indicator/number-of-nursing-facility-beds/
36 Centers for Medicare & Medicaid Services, Office of the Actuary, National Health Statistics Group, https://www.cms.gov/Research-Statistics-Data-and-Sys-tems/Statistics-Trends-and-Reports/NationalHealthExpendData/downloads/proj2010.pdf

Maybe Morningstar's estimates are wrong[37] and 40% of those over age 65 WON'T require Facility-Based care at some point in their life, and 10% of those individuals WON'T require care for 5 year or more. If Morningstar's estimates are even partially accurate, simple math tells you by 2020 the country will be in need of approximately 500,000 additional beds. At that point, it won't matter what government programs cover if the 68% of "for-profit" facilities simply choose not participate! *That's the Economic Reality of Long-Term Care!*

Dan McGrath, Director of Institutional Marketing at Zenith Marketing Group sums up the situation, saying Long-Term Care Planning "*is no longer about protecting assets in retirement; it has become the best negotiating chip one can have to access care in retirement.*"[38]

Now that you've read this book to this point, hopefully you will take a pragmatic view of the future delivery of healthcare and Long-Term Care services. I encourage you to embrace the fact that the basic law of supply and demand will likely have far greater impact on the cost, choice and availability of healthcare, than most people realize today.

---

37 Christine Benz, Morningstar, "*40 Must-Know Statistics About Long-Term Care*", August 9, 2012

38 INERTIA / Advisor Services Group, "*Long-Term Care: The Economic Reality*", June 19, 2013

How Do I Start The Long-Term Care Planning Process?

When discussing Long-Term Care planning, most consumers tend to focus only on asset protection, rather than the valuable benefits of actually having a Long-Term Care Plan.

Long-Term Care planning is often a very emotional process for people. Understanding the need to evaluate and consider a Long-Term Care plan is an important first step. The next step is to begin the conversation with a spouse, family member or loved one and include your individual needs and concerns early in the conversation. Doing so will make it easier to implement an appropriate plan and better understand the planning process. Here are a few process-driven tips to consider as you move forward:

Put some thought into it

Before the planning process begins, consider the following question: "*Why do most people implement a Long-Term Care plan?*"

A few of the most common reasons include:

1. To avoid burdening loved ones with caregiving roles.
2. To have greater choice of where they receive care.
3. To maintain control over important care decisions.
4. To remain in their own home, and receive care there.

Have a conversation

During the fact-finding process, isolate the most important reason for implementing a Long-Term Care plan. Here are a few sample questions I like to include in my discussions:

- *"What is the primary reason YOU are considering Long-Term Care planning?"*

- *"If there comes a day where YOU need Long-Term Care, what are the most important items YOUR plan should address?"*

- *"We all face questions about our care and independence as we age. What is YOUR biggest concern should YOU need Long-Term Care?"*

Understand How A Long-Term Care Plan Claim Is Triggered

Long-Term Care services, as previously mentioned, can be received in a variety of settings. Once your Long-Term Care plan is implemented, your plan's benefits will be available to you in the event you go "on claim", or when the normal activities you do without help can no longer be done. These are called activities of daily living (ADLs), or a cognitive impairment, and include bathing, continence, dressing, eating, toileting, and transferring. The inability to perform two of the six (ADLs) is what gives you the ability to trigger a claim.

Customized Plan Design

By understanding the motivation *behind* the reasons to plan for future Long-Term Care needs, it's much easier to begin the process of tailoring a Long-Term Care plan with appropriate solutions. This can be simple for some people, and for others it can be more complicated. In any event, recognizing the non-financial benefits of a customized Long-Term Care plan is when most people find that their plan becomes a key component of their comprehensive financial plan.

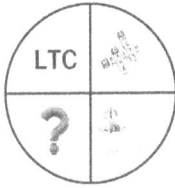

What Are The Solutions for Long-Term Care Planning?

When building any structure, the key to it standing the test of time is a solid foundation. The same is true when implementing a Long-Term Care plan.

For example, it's entirely possible to have two houses, side by side, and from the outside they look nearly identical. However, what can't be seen is that one has a fully finished basement and the other sits on a slab without a basement. With respect to Long-Term Care planning, don't make the mistake of looking from the outside and assuming that all plans are the same.

There are a number of steps to take before implementing a Long-Term Care plan, including plan design (blueprints), selecting the proper benefit model (foundation) and selecting the proper solutions (structure). Unfortunately, many consumers and advisors see only the blueprints or the structure, without even a cursory look at the benefit model, or foundation, of the plan.

This multi-step process is another reason why Long-Term Care planning should be a detailed process and not simply a product to be purchased. Consider the three basic foundations for a Long-Term Care plan (below) to help you better understand how these affect the plan you might eventually implement. Knowing how these models differ will allow for the customization of a plan that works as intended and provide peace of mind for years to come.

Reimbursement Plans

Under this type of plan, Long-Term Care benefits will be reimbursed for qualified expenses, as the actual bills are submitted and processed. For example, if someone submits a claim, with a $250/day limit for plan benefits, the bills will be submitted and reimbursed up to that $250 limit. Reimbursement plans are also available with a monthly limit, where a $250/day benefit, using a monthly benefit multiplier, would provide a plan with $7,500 per month in benefits available for qualified expenses.

Qualifying expenses, under a reimbursement model, usually do not include things like home modification, medical equipment (i.e. walkers) or many other potential expenses associated with a Long-Term Care need. When selecting a Long-Term Care plan built on the foundation of a reimbursement benefit model, it's very important to note what expenses are usually covered, and whether those benefits are paid on a daily versus monthly maximum. This is especially important in a comprehensive Long-Term Care plan, where some levels of care (i.e. Alzheimer's care) might exceed the limitations of the plan.

Indemnity Plans

Under this type of plan, Long-Term Care benefits are paid to the claimant based on the daily or monthly limits, however there is no requirement to submit actual bills once the claim is initiated.

Now let's consider the same $250/day or $7,500/month scenario that we used for a reimbursement plan.

The primary difference is that it doesn't matter how much the actual charges might be, the claimant will receive the *stipulated* amount up to the plan limits. Some plans may require a licensed service provider to be involved in the care; however no bills or receipts are needed to justify the cost of care. There are some solutions that call for monthly or annual re-verification of services, or require copies of bills be submitted to prove continued use of a licensed provider.

The cautionary point with the indemnity model is that while it seems simple to access benefits, it may expend the available benefit pool more quickly. Also, since Long-Term Care plan benefits are usually received income tax-free, it's important to know the exact federal limitation on how much can be received to stay under the threshold.

Stepped-Up Income Plans

There are a number of new options, such as Asset-Based Long-Term Care solutions, which can be incorporated with a retirement income plan, to provide a "*stepped-up*" amount of income should Long-Term Care be needed. Some provide a step-up for nursing home care only, while other plans have separate step-up benefits depending on the actual level of care needed.

For example, under normal circumstances, someone with one of these Asset-Based solutions might receive $1,500 per month in guaranteed income. However, should that individual qualify for the Long-Term Care benefit under the plan, the income payment could step-up to as much as $3,000 per month.

I often recommend this type of solution when we use a multi-tiered approach to a Long-Term Care plan, or if someone has a health issue which would disqualify him or her from other solutions. In most cases, this type of benefit model might allow someone to augment their primary Long-Term Care plan by using IRA or 401(k) assets.

It's important to note that accessing a Long-Term Care plan set up with IRA or 401(k) dollars will result in the benefits becoming "ordinary income" and taxed as such. However, the ability to step-up income can be a significant benefit for a spouse/partner relying on the initial guaranteed income stream.

What Are The Basic Options for Long-Term Care Plans?

A customized Long-Term Care plan can use a variety of solutions, including a single solution or possibly even multiple "layered" solutions. However, there are generally five basic types of solutions:

1. Traditional Long-Term Care insurance

2. Long-Term Care / Life Insurance Hybrids

3. Annuity / Long-Term Care Hybrids

4. Life Insurance with a Long-Term Care or Chronic Illness rider

5. Annuities with income riders for nursing home confinement

Each has different features and benefits, which we'll address, but all of them generally cover various Long-Term Care services. Before going into detail about each of these options, it's important to understand the components of each plan and some terminology.

Plan design basics

Benefit Amount: This is the daily or monthly amount covered by a plan, and specified when the insurance is applied for.

Benefit Period or Multiplier: This is the period of time during which the benefit amount will be paid, and will range from 1 year to as long as for your lifetime.

Elimination Period: This is much like a deductible, and it is the time period which must elapse after you are certified by a physician to need Long-Term Care services. This will range from 0 to 365 days.

Inflation Protection: With healthcare costs continuing to rise over time, inflation protection will increase your Benefit Amount on an annual basis. Insurance carriers offer a variety of inflation protection options to choose from, so it's important to understand how this plan component works.

Shared Care/Coverage: This option allows both spouses/partners to share each other's benefit period. For instance, if each person has a four year benefit period, then the total benefit period available to be "shared" is eight years.

Waiver of Premium: This feature waives the premiums being paid on the policy once you begin receiving benefits.

Return/Refund of Premium: This feature allows you to have your premiums returned in the event you pass away or, in some cases, decide to terminate your plan.

Features & Benefits:

Care Coordination Services: Many LTC policies provide assistance in planning your Long-Term Care services when you need care. They assess your functional and cognitive capabilities along with your personal need for care and services. Then they work with you to identify the specific services and care providers that you will need. Additionally, they will develop and recommend, the initial and future "Plan of Care", ensure initial and ongoing eligibility certifications and even help complete claim forms.

Restoration of Benefits: If you begin receiving benefits from your plan, and fully recover for a specified period of time, the carrier will "restore" all or a portion of the original benefits.

Nonforfeiture Benefit: If, for some reason, your policy lapses and it's been in-force for a specified period, the carrier will provide you with a reduced, paid-up benefit, and the specifics vary by carrier.

Bed Reservation: This benefit pays to reserve your room or bed for any reason while you are temporarily absent from your stay in a covered facility.

1) Traditional Long-Term Care Insurance Plans

Once you understand the basic plan design features and benefit, you can begin to look at how those are incorporated into the various solutions. The oldest, and first consideration for many people, tends to be what we call, traditional Long-Term Care insurance plans. This will look and feel much like home or auto insurance, where you pay a specific cost or premium, to cover a specific amount of coverage.

Plan design flexibility

Long-Term Care insurance solutions have evolved over time, and today provide the most flexible way to design a Long-Term Care plan. While it may be the most flexible, that flexibility carries a price. Long-Term Care insurance, like home or auto insurance, provides "use it or lose it" benefits, so generally it will have no residual value if Long-Term Care is never needed. Essentially all of those dollars paid over the years will have gone down the drain if you don't use the benefits. If this doesn't bother you, and you want access to all the bells & whistles, then Long-Term Care insurance may be a good option to consider.

In addition to a lack of residual value, another drawback to Long-Term Care insurance is the fact that plan costs are not guaranteed. While the cost of Long-Term Care insurance might look like an affordable plan design option today, that cost could, and likely will, increase in the future. If cost certainty in your Long-Term Care plan is important, you may want to consider other options.

Talking taxes

Long-Term Care insurance, unlike other options, may provide tax benefits for you too. Depending on where you live, premiums paid for Long-Term Care insurance may be eligible for an income tax deduction. The amount of the deduction often depends on your age. Additionally, benefits paid from Long-Term Care insurance are generally excluded from income.

If you're a business owner, your business may be able to deduct the cost of premiums, but generally corporations paying premiums for an employee are 100% deductible if not included in employee's taxable income.[39]

---

39 Always check with your tax provider on these points!

Plan funding

Long-Term Care insurance policies today are generally paid for on a regular basis for life; either annually, semi-annually, quarterly or monthly. In the past, it was possible to "pay-up" a policy early, like a "10-pay" or "paid-up at 65" scenario, but these options have almost disappeared from the market.

2) Long-Term Care / Life Insurance Hybrids

Most people understand life insurance; you pay the premiums, and your policy pays a death benefit when you pass away. It's a pretty simple concept.

The Long-Term Care / Life Insurance hybrid solution combines life insurance *with* a Long-Term Care policy, and it is quickly becoming a very popular planning solution.

Plan design flexibility

The hybrids were once somewhat bland solutions, but today they can be almost as flexible as Long-Term Care insurance and provide many, if not all, of the features and benefits.

A huge difference with these solutions is that one way or another there WILL be a benefit paid out from a Long-Term Care / Life Insurance hybrid. Either in the form of Long-Term Care benefit or a death benefit, versus traditional Long-Term Care insurance where there will not be a benefit if Long-Term Care is never needed.

In addition to addressing residual value, Long-Term Care / Life Insurance hybrids can build cost certainty into your Long Time Care plan, as the premiums are generally fixed and guaranteed for life.

Talking taxes

Premiums for Long-Term Care / Life Insurance hybrids will not be eligible for an income tax deduction, because unlike Long-Term Care insurance, there is a tax-free death benefit included. The benefits paid from the plan, just like Long-Term Care insurance, are generally excluded from income.

If you're a business owner, there are a variety of ways to take advantage of these solutions, but I recommend that you work with a Long-Term Care Planning specialist to determine what is best for your particular situation.[40]

Plan funding

This is where Long-Term Care / Life Insurance hybrids really get interesting. Just like traditional life insurance, Long-Term Care / Life Insurance hybrid solutions offer the most flexible funding options of any plan type. They can be paid ongoing, in a short-pay scenario, all at once and even offer you the ability to upgrade your existing life insurance (we will discuss this later) into a hybrid solution.

3) Life Insurance with a Long-Term Care or Chronic Illness Rider

So, you're thinking, "*what the difference between this solution and a Long-Term Care / Life Insurance hybrid*"? Actually, quite a bit!!

Without getting into the specifics, there's a different section of the tax code, which applies to this type of solution. Plus, most Long-Term Care / Life Insurance hybrid solutions are based on a "reimbursement" benefit models which we

---

40 You may find a LTC Planning specialist here: http://www.WhatsTheDealWith-LTC.com/contact-us/

discussed earlier, while most Long-Term Care/ Chronic Illness Rider solutions provide "indemnity" benefits.

Plan design flexibility

There are a number of reasons the Long-Term Care/ Chronic Illness Rider solutions are becoming more popular today, and how they can easily fit into your comprehensive planning. Primarily, they are very basic solutions, as the death benefit can be tapped for "living benefits" for Long-Term Care needs.

If the life insurance contract is set up properly, the cost can be fixed and guaranteed for life, with benefits available up to age 120. Since the Long-Term Care benefits are based on the death benefit, it's also possible to have a growing death benefit, as the accumulating cash value can organically push the death benefit higher over time.

Lastly, underwriting requirements for life insurance solutions are based on mortality, or life expectancy, where solutions geared more towards Long-Term Care are under-written based more on morbidity, or disease/illness.

Talking taxes

Premiums for Long-Term Care/ Chronic Illness Rider will not be eligible for an income tax deduction, because unlike Long-Term Care Insurance, there is a tax-free death benefit included. The benefits paid from the plan, under current tax law, are generally excluded from income up to certain federal limitations.

If you're a business owner, there are a variety of ways to take advantage of these solutions, but we recommend that you work with a Long-Term Care Planning specialist to determine what is best for your particular situation.

Plan funding

Just like traditional life insurance, Long-Term Care/ Chronic Illness Rider offer very most flexible funding options for your plan. Premiums can be paid ongoing, in a short-pay scenario, or all at once and they can even offer you the ability to upgrade your existing life insurance.

4) Annuity/Long-Term Care Hybrid

Annuities have been around in one form or another since the Roman Empire.[41] It's time to forget what your neighbor, or some media pundit, told you or wrote about annuities as they've now become a staple of financial planning.

Many people understand how annuities allow you to put your money in a vehicle, which will grow tax-deferred over time, and then allow you to use those dollars as supplemental retirement income if needed. What most people don't know is how to use annuities for Long-Term Care planning as well!

Plan design flexibility

Annuity/Long-Term Care hybrids have not been around as long as their Life Insurance/ Long-Term Care hybrid siblings, but because of recent changes in the tax code they are becoming a very appropriate Long-Term Care plan design option for many people.

Annuity/Long-Term Care hybrids are basic is their plan design format; some amount goes in, and some amount of benefit is provided for Long-Term Care needs. But, in 2006 Congress passed the Pension Protection Act (PPA), which gave these hybrids some serious advantages. [42]

---

41 Wikipedia, "Annuity History", http://en.wikipedia.org/wiki/Annuity_(US_financial_products)

42 OneAmerica, *"What you need to know about the Pension Protection Act, annuities and long-term care protection"*, http://www.assetbasedltc.com/Pension-Protection-Act-Long-Term-Care-Benefits.php

Typically, distributions from annuities are what we call LIFO or "last in, first out". This means that all of the gains or interest earned is paid out first, and are taxable in the year taken, until you reach your "basis" or original deposit. Today's PPA compliant annuities are VERY different when it comes to Long-Term Care benefits, as all of the gains in your annuity can be distributed **tax-free** to cover Long-Term Care expenses.

Talking taxes

There isn't a tax benefit for moving funds going into an Annuity/Long-Term Care hybrid, but with today's low interest rate environment, the ability to earn up to three times the rate of CDs or money market accounts, in a tax-deferred vehicle, and using the accumulation tax-free for Long-Term Care expenses can be a big plus!

Plan funding

Annuity/Long-Term Care hybrids are funded with a single premium, or with the accumulated cash value of an existing fixed or variable annuity or life insurance contract. If it's a non-qualified contract, you have the ability to upgrade the existing contract into a PPA compliant Long-Term Care Annuity.

5) Annuities with Income Riders?

OK, so again you're thinking, "*what the difference between this solution and an Annuity/Long-Term Care hybrid*"? And again, quite a bit!!

Primarily, these are **very** basic Long-Term Care solutions, and most only provide benefits for actual nursing home confinement. The way the benefits are provided is also unique, in the fact that these annuity solutions are designed to provide lifetime income, and in the event of nursing home confinement, the income level will be increased by some predetermined amount, for some predetermined time period.

Plan design flexibility

Since the benefits of these annuity solutions are usually for confinement only, I recommend using these solutions as a supplementary component in a "Layered" Long-Term Care plan and not as a consumer's primary component of their Long-Term Care plan. These solutions are flexible in the sense that, depending on the funding source (which we'll get into more detail shortly) the accumulating assets may continue to grow indefinitely. This growth will eventually determine your income of Long-Term Care benefits.

Additionally, these solutions are available for individuals with a variety of risk tolerances. For those with little risk tolerance there are fixed interest solutions, which guarantee a specified insurance carrier with declared interest crediting to your annuity.

Second, you can consider Indexed Annuities, which generally provide "capped", market-linked interest crediting based on stock market indexes, but cannot be less than 0%.

Lastly, there are Variable Annuities, with uncapped interest crediting based positively and negatively on underlying mutual fund sub-accounts.

Talking taxes

Premiums for these solutions will not be eligible for an income tax deduction, unless it's an IRA contribution. Additionally, the income benefits to help pay for Long-Term Care will be fully taxable in the year taken.

Plan funding

This is what makes Annuities with Income Riders a unique solution.

According to recent statistics, Americans have more than $17 TRILLION in retirement assets and another $1.6 TRILLION of assets in annuities.[43] However, it's nearly impossible to use those dollars to fund a Long-Term Care plan without creating a taxable event.

Since you may have a large amount of your personal net-worth tied up in retirement accounts or annuities, repositioning some of those dollars and addressing potential Long-Term Care needs can make perfect sense for many. Funding these solutions is almost always done with a one-time deposit, transferring of retirement account dollars or by upgrading an existing annuity.

---

43 Statistica, "*Total assets of retirement annuities in the U.S. from 2000 to 2011 (in billion U.S. dollars)*", http://www.statista.com/statistics/188002/retirement-annuities-total-assets-in-the-us-since-2000/

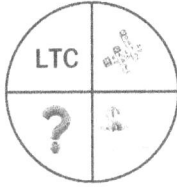

What's The Next Step In The Long-Term Care Planning Process?

Now that you are here, you should have a better understanding of Long-Term Care planning basics than the majority of the general public.

Unfortunately, understanding what you've read isn't really going to give you the ability to move forward independently. Your Long-Term Care plan may have a number of moving parts, and needs to be working in concert with any other planning you've done or are considering.

The next step is to sit down with an advisor who can help you navigate the plan design phase, and who has access to all of the available solutions we've discussed. As a cautionary note, you may be surprised that your current advisor may not be the most appropriate one to move forward with, as many are unable to discuss, or offer you Long-Term Care plan options.

Why do the large financial services firms ignore Long-Term Care Planning?

The financial services community isn't going to appreciate what I'm about to tell you, but if you're working with an advisor at one of the country's largest firms, you should realize that the possibility exists that most are NOT prepared to discuss Long-Term Care planning with you.

It's probably a good idea to take a step back and look at an event, which occurred in the late 1990's. Prior to Congress passing the Gramm–Leach–Bliley Act of 1999, there were strict rules prohibiting affiliations between banks, brokerage and insurance companies set forth by the Glass–Steagall Act, the term applied to the Banking Act of 1933. [44]

Most of this was a result of what occurred in 1997, when Citigroup grew out of the combination of Smith Barney, Travelers and Citibank. This created one of the first "financial supermarkets", capable of cross-selling insurance, investments and banking products to an ever-growing customer base. Not to be outdone, State Farm, the "*nation's largest Auto and Home insurer serving 28 million households…and the second largest life insurance company in the U.S.*" took a similar approach.

In 1998, State Farm got into the game and gave their business model a makeover—State Farm Bank was born!! Then, in 2001, recognizing the ongoing demographic shift and continued importance of retirement planning by their Boomer clients, State Farm began marketing and selling their own family of mutual funds and now has over "*$11 billion in mutual*

---

44 Wikipedia, "*1933 Banking Act*", http://en.wikipedia.org/wiki/Banking_Act_of_1933

fund assets under management," and nearly *another $10 billion in deposits in State Farm Bank.*[45]

Other companies followed suit to effectively tap their existing client base to maximize their client relationships.

However, some fifteen or so years later we've basically come full circle. Firms and advisors are now focused on their core competencies more than ever—providing advice, yes, but their solutions are mainly based on investments and managed money.

With respect to Long-Term Care planning and the solutions we've outlined, the problem with the country's largest firms comes from the top, and goes all the way to the advisor, because these solution now make up an inconsequential portion of their total business. So, rather than acknowledge that their clients need to consider Long-Term Care planning, and make this an area of importance, they tend to merely provide access to some solutions and hope their advisors get by with a small selection of predetermined products.

Another problem for the largest firms is that many of these solutions create a "turf war", as many of today's Long-Term Care planning solutions cross over the various product lines among the departments. In fact, one of the largest financial services firms in the country will not use a particular carrier's solutions, because ***internally*** they cannot figure out which business unit should be credited for promoting them. Without specifically naming the guilty, we'll give you an example of what we're talking about.

---

45 Federal Deposit Insurance Corporation, "State Farm Bank, FSB", http://www2.fdic.gov/sod/sodInstBranchRpt.asp?rCert=34617&baritem=1&ryear=2011

I worked on one case recently for a couple, where "Steve" is 55 years old, and "Sally" is 60. They've spent the last twenty years running the business Steve's father originally started; a business, which they desire to have run by their children when they retire. Steve and Sally have seen, first hand, the erosion of 75 years of hard-earned savings due to Long-Term Care expenses, as Steve's father suffered from Alzheimer's for the last 12 years of his life. His father's illness took a physical and emotional toll on Steve's mother, and it had a serious impact on her ability to maintain her lifestyle. Especially once she began paying for Alzheimer's care, which in a nursing home setting, routinely exceeded $10,000 per month.

The couple wanted to include a Long-Term Care component to their financial plan, but they insisted the plan include four distinct features.

1. Short Pay—*The plan must be fully funded in 10 years, when Steve retires.*

2. Lifetime Benefits—*The plan should provide benefits for as long as LONG-TERM CARE is needed.*

3. Inflation Protection—*It should have increasing benefits to address rising healthcare costs.*

4. Return of Premium—*Every dollar spent should come back to their estate if they don't need LONG-TERM CARE.*

The couple had a good relationship with Advisor A, who works at a very well-known firm. He included Long-Term Care Planning as part of the couple's semi-annual review. However, after doing a search of his firm's **approved** solutions, Advisor A informed the couple there wasn't one which fit their desired parameters.

Advisor A recommended the couple re-evaluate their Long-Term Care planning needs and be more "realistic" with their expectations, and then he felt it might be possible to then identify a Long-Term Care solution which could work. The review continued and the Long-Term Care topic was tabled for a later date. Later that day, Sally discussed the situation with Steve and neither wanted to "re-evaluate" their Long-Term Care planning parameters; they wanted a second opinion.

The next day, Sally contacted Advisor B, who was referred to her by a friend who recently implemented a Long-Term Care plan. Advisor B also works with another very well know firm, but partners with my firm for her clients' Long-Term Care planning needs. With all of the pertinent information gathered from Sally, it was passed to my team and we found a number of options which met Steve & Sally's demands. A meeting was set with Steve & Sally to discuss the solutions we identified. Once the options were explained, the decision was fairly simple and we began the process of implementing the couple's Long-Term Care plan.

While things worked out well for Steve, Sally and Advisor B; the same could not be said for Advisor A.

Steve could not understand why Advisor A, working for such a large and well-known firm, didn't have access to the same planning solutions we presented. After explaining some of the reasons, Steve was concerned that there might be other aspects of their investment and insurance portfolio, which needed to be reviewed. Within a month, Steve and Sally had moved all of their investments—*Totaling more than $3,000,000*—to Advisor B!

Should I do an insurance and annuity review for my Long-Term Care Planning?

Once you've decided on the advisor to work with to design your Long-Term Care plan, it's critically important to review your entire insurance and annuity portfolio in the process. But don't forget to include Medicare Supplements, health insurance and property & casualty insurance!!

As you age, you are going to find your insurance needs change and an insurance review should be completed regularly. While the importance of insurance will continue, repositioning your insurance portfolio should be done with an eye towards retirement. From a retirement planning perspective it should be an absolute requirement to review life insurance & annuities. It may seem obvious, but many people forget to do simple things such as updating beneficiaries and coverage even after significant life events occur.

With respect to Long-Term Care planning, the reality is that today's life insurance and annuity solution allow many people to upgrade their insurance portfolio AND plan for potential Long-Term Care needs.....often with little or no out of pocket cost!!

How Do I Begin the Insurance Review Process?

There are a variety of factors to consider during a review, but it should NOT be done solely to lower your total insurance cost. The review process should be done to determine how to best incorporate various insurance solutions into a comprehensive financial plan.

Be prepared by gathering all of pertinent documents, including policies, declaration pages, recent statements and wills/trusts to begin the process. Be sure to determine what the goals are, as this will help meet planning expectations. A thorough insurance review should look at all existing insurance, including life, disability, Long-Term Care, annuities and even property and casualty. Once the review is completed, it is then possible to determine if changes should be made, and how the changes will better position someone for the future.

When doing the review, adding a Long-Term Care component may further complicate matters, and that's a primary reason to work with a knowledgeable advisor throughout the process. Not only does another set of eyes help with the review process, but in the long run they may be able to identify options that you weren't even aware of. As the marketplace for Long-Term Care solutions continues to evolve, it's very important that a Long-Term Care Plan will stand the test of time. After all, it may be decades until it's put in motion.

Can I Turn taxable dollars into tax-free benefits for Long-Term Care needs?

April 15th is just one of those dates Americans would like to skip!

Each and every year, you dig out your records to complete the task of filing your taxes, and each year it's likely that you review your retirement and annuity account statements, and you're not the only one paying attention!! The IRS can't wait for you to start spending your retirement dollars so that taxes on that money to begin rolling into the Treasury. If you think you're interested in seeing those accounts grow, just imagine the anticipation the IRS has of getting a piece of the action when it becomes income.

While it's very difficult, if not impossible, to avoid paying taxes on distributions from retirement accounts and annuities, there are strategies to consider which may make the impending tax bill a bit more palatable. This is especially true in the context of your Long-Term Care planning, as there are a variety of ways you can effectively turn taxable dollars into *tax-free benefits*. Before getting to that discussion, let's look at two primary issues with respect to retirement accounts and annuities.

When you begin taking distributions from retirement accounts, it's usually done in conjunction with receiving Social Security. While Social Security benefits may or may not be fully taxable, retirement plan distributions WILL be fully taxable. Once retirees understand this, some try to delay taking taxable distributions of their retirement accounts; however this tactic only delays the inevitable. Like it or not, at age 70 ½, the government requires retirement accounts begin being tapped through Required Minimum Distributions (RMDs).[46] Without some prudent planning, this means a retiree's tax bill may actually go up during retirement.

There's another reason Uncle Sam loves your retirement accounts—*You're human and your clock is ticking*.

There are significant tax implications for retirement accounts, which are passed on to non-spousal beneficiaries. Every situation is unique, and you should get specific guidance from a tax professional or CPA, but generally speaking, the IRS is always going to their cut one way or another.

---

46 United Stated Department of the Treasury, Internal Revenue Service, "*Retirement Plans FAQs regarding Required Minimum Distributions*", Last Reviewed or Updated: February 6, 2013

The Reality of Tax-Deferred Annuities

The dollars, which are taxed, or those remaining to cover living expenses and savings, are referred to as "*non-qualified*" dollars. Many people use a portion of those non-qualified dollars to create supplemental retirement plans, which will augment Social Security benefits and their retirement accounts distributions.

With the previously mentioned $1.6 Trillion dollars in non-qualified annuities,[47] it's clear the tax-deferral features of these solutions are appealing. However, only 10% of all "non-qualified" annuities are actually tapped for income needs, and the other 90% will continue to grow until the owner of the annuity passes away. What happens then? The beneficiary listed on the account receives the proceeds of the annuity, *along with a 1099 some months later to include when they prepare their taxes*.

How Can Long-Term Care Planning Make These Situations Better?

The answer to this question is going to depend on numerous variables, and for those willing to take the time, they will find a variety of planning options. Perhaps the best feature to Long-Term Care planning is that most of today's solutions provide TAX-FREE benefits to pay for care.

Here are two real life examples I've discussed recently with advisors and their clients...

---

47 ibid

#1—Long-Term Care Planning utilizing retirement assets

After meeting to discuss Long-Term Care planning, and potentially appropriate solutions, for a client, I focused on a large IRA that was not being used for retirement income. The clients were approaching 70 ½ and will soon begin taking RMDs totaling roughly $15,000 per year. Based on their age, traditional Long-Term Care insurance could be purchased with a portion of this income stream, but that doesn't eliminate the problem of the tax bill headed to the children when the balance of the IRA is passed onto them.

In this situation, the recommended solution involved the implementation of a Long-Term Care plan using a Life Insurance/Long-Term Care hybrid solution. Taxes would be paid annually on the distributions to fund their Long-Term Care plans, just as would be the case with any RMDs, but the life insurance benefit is a key component.

If Long-Term Care were needed, the couple would have a substantial TAX-FREE benefit stream to utilize. If Long-Term Care were not needed, the life insurance benefit would pass to the children TAX-FREE; helping them pay the taxes due on the remaining IRA balance. Effectively, this solution helps turn various taxable dollars into TAX-FREE dollars for the beneficiaries and for future Long-Term Care needs.

#2—Putting Those Non-Qualified Annuities To Work

Another situation we encountered recently was a widower, age 62, with annuities purchased over the years; now valued at approximately $250,000. This individual didn't need additional income, and wasn't taking distributions from the annuities, yet he planned to use the annuities to pay for Long-Term Care expenses in the future.

By using the tax code to his advantage—*specifically the previously mentioned Pension Protection Act (PPA) of 2006*[48]—we showed him a way to "upgrade" his annuities into a PPA compliant solution. This individual invested approximately $125,000 (basis) into his annuities, which means there was about $125,000 in gains. Taking distributions to pay for Long-Term Care expenses, from his existing annuities, would result in reportable income in the year it is taken. However, "upgrading" to the PPA compliant solutions would not result in a taxable event, and any future distributions to cover qualified Long-Term Care expenses would be TAX-FREE.

While there may be tax implications to his beneficiaries if Long-Term Care isn't needed (*just like there would be in the old annuities),* the PPA compliant solution effectively turns taxable dollars into TAX-FREE dollars for future Long-Term Care needs. As you review your retirement accounts and annuities, think about the tax implications not next April 15th, but on "tax day" at some point in the future. If Long-Term Care planning has yet to be addressed, consider making that a priority and, by all means, use the tax code to your advantage!!

Finding A Long-Term Care Planning Specialist

This is where things can get very tricky! You may work with a variety of advisors, but it's unlikely that any of them will be well versed on the topic of Long-Term Care Planning. Even if you're satisfied with your current advisory relationship(s), that

---

48 ibid

doesn't mean your advisor(s) is/are prepared to handle the implementation of your Long-Term Care Plan.

Here are some questions to pose to him/her to determine if they're truly prepared to help you and your family with Long-Term Care planning. If they can't answer these questions quickly and easily, you may want to consider working with an advisor who is more focused on Long-Term Care planning:

1. In the past 12 months, how many clients have you implemented a Long-Term Care plan for?

2. How can I use the Pension Protection Act of 2006 to implement my Long-Term Care plan?

3. How might you consider repositioning my existing insurance/annuities for Long-Term Care planning?

4. Other than traditional Long-Term Care insurance, how many other types of Long-Term Care solutions do you usually recommend?

5. If I want to build cost certainty into a Long-Term Care plan, and guarantee my plan will provide benefits at some point in time, what solutions can you provide to accomplish my goal?

Conclusion regarding Long-Term Care Planning

Clearly, there is more to Long-Term Care planning than simply buying a product! I've tried to lay out the basics for you, and it's probably going to take some time for it to all sink in. That being said, don't procrastinate and begin the process too late because your age and health will become a bigger factor (often a negative factor) in your decision making process.

In whatever form your Long-Term Care plan takes, it's going to be part of your comprehensive planning for a very long time; so do it right! Take the knowledge that I've given you and reach out to a trusted advisor who can help you understand and implement the right solution for you and your family.

Long-Term Care Resources

Visit

www.WhatsTheDealWithLTC.com
for more information and assistance in
finding an advisor to help you with your
Long-Term Care Planning needs.

Also, visit Mike Padawer's company site at
http://www.inertia-asg.com
for more information
on Long-Term Care
with resources for
individuals, advisors and
institutions

Helpful Resources For Long-Term Care Planning:

- **INERTIA / Advisor Services Group**: http://www.inertia-asg.com

- **U.S. Department of Health and Human Services**: http://longtermcare.gov

- **Social Security Administration**: http://www.ssa.gov

- **Veterans Administration**: http://www.va.gov/geriatrics/

- **The Life and Health Insurance Foundation for Education**: http://www.lifehappens.org/long-term-care-insurance-introduction/

- **Kiplinger**: http://kiplingers.com/fronts/special-report/long-term-care-insurance/index.html

- **Alzheimer's Association**: http://www.alz.org/care/alzheimers-dementia-financial-legal-planning.asp

- **3 in 4 Need More**: http://www.3in4needmore.com/about/

- **The National Resource Center on LGBT Aging**: http://www.lgbtagingcenter.org/index.cfm

- **AARP**: http://www.aarp.org/relationships/caregiving/info-10-2009/women_planning_retirement.html?intc-mp=outbrain&obref=obinsite

- **John Hancock, Cost of Care Calculator**: http://www.johnhancockltc.com/individual/cost-of-long-term-care-calculator/index.html

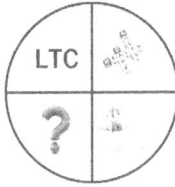

About Mike Padawer

Mike Padawer has more than two decades of experience in the financial services arena; including roles in retail, wholesale and sales management functions. Today, he focuses solely on working with advisors and institutions; providing customized Long-Term Care planning solutions for their individual, group and business owner clients.

Mike works diligently with his advisor partners and their clients, to help transfer the potentially catastrophic risk and burden of Long-Term Care needs, away from the individual and their families.

Regardless of the audience, Mike believes that educating the client about future Long-Term Care needs, and understanding their unique circumstance, is paramount to implementing planning which will stand the test of time.

Mike's background also includes successful implementation of training, coaching and Continuing Education programs which have helped hundreds of advisors meet the financial planning needs of their clients.

Mike resides in Chesterfield, Missouri. He enjoys live music, playing golf and ice hockey, and traveling with his children.

Mike Padawer

President

INERTIA / Advisor Services Group

mike.padawer@inertia-asg.com

Bus: 314.757.8625

Fax: 888.757.4274

www.ingramcontent.com/pod-product-compliance
Lightning Source LLC
Chambersburg PA
CBHW050606280326
41933CB00011B/2003